Stars

BY **Steve Tomecek**

ILLUSTRATED BY **Sachiko Yoshikawa**

NATIONAL GEOGRAPHIC

WASHINGTON, D.C.

To my sister Marianne,
who's always been one of my shining stars!—ST

To Munetada, Yoko, Nancy, and
my dearest husband, Wayne—SY

Look up at the stars on a clear dark night....
It's amazing how many you can see. Choose one
star and make a wish.

Have you ever wondered where stars go in the daytime?
Why stars shine so bright in the night?
What stars are made of?

Come along with us to learn all about stars!

If you want to see stars, you have to wait until it gets dark. Where do stars go in the daytime? Nowhere! Even though you can't see them, stars are still shining in the sky.

The shining sun makes the sky so bright that starlight can't be seen. As the sun begins to set, the sky gets darker. Then one by one the stars start to appear.

cock-a-doodle-doo!

Sometimes, even at night,
it's hard for you to see the stars.
That's especially true if you live in a
city where there are many bright lights.
This is because the lights act like
the sun. They make the sky
too bright for you to see the stars.

中華飯店

HOTEL

8

Out in the country, far from the city,
there are fewer bright lights.
Here you can really see the stars.
They look like they go on forever.

What do stars look like?
Sometimes people draw stars with little points.
But real stars don't have points. They are
round, just like our sun. In fact, our sun is a star.
It's our star, the closest one to Earth.

Even though stars look like little dots, they are huge. Just like our sun, they are gigantic balls of hot, glowing gas. So why do stars look so much smaller than our sun? It's because they are much farther away.

From here on Earth, our sun looks like the biggest,
brightest star. But compared to many other stars,
our sun is small. It only looks very big to us because
it is much closer to Earth than other stars.

If you could get on a rocket ship and fly away from our sun, the sun would look like it's getting smaller and smaller. When you were really far away, our sun would look just like a little dot. It would look just like the stars you see in the night sky.

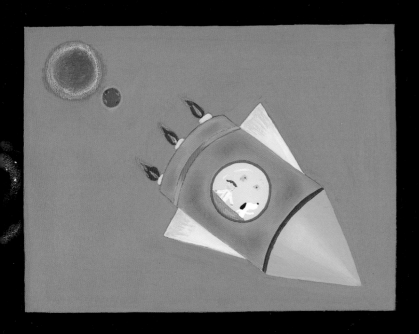

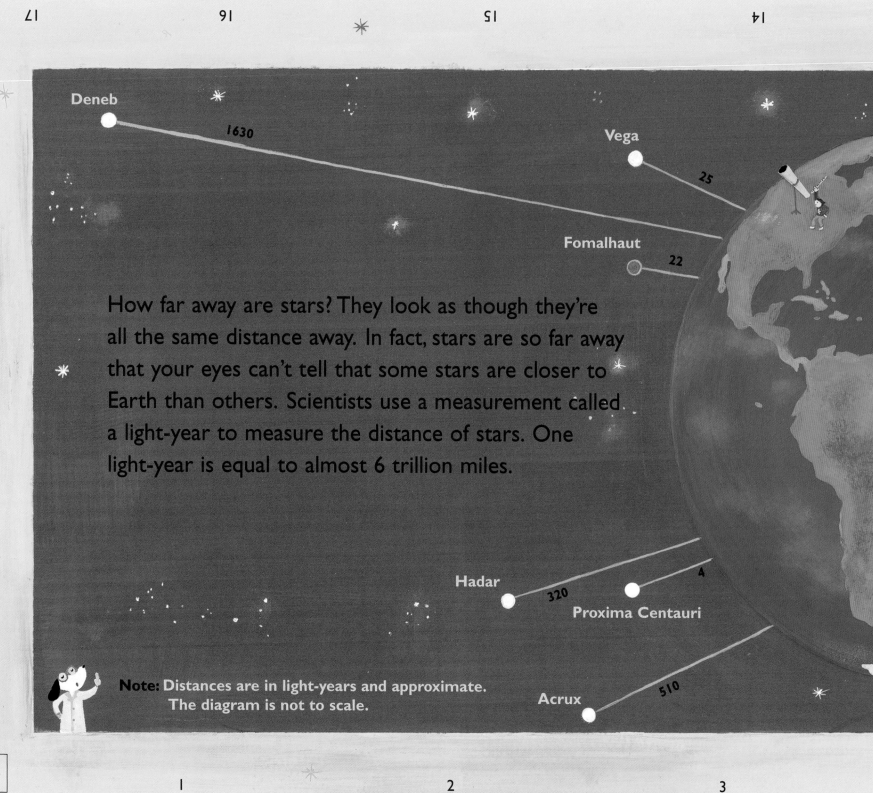

Deneb

1630

Vega

25

Fomalhaut

22

How far away are stars? They look as though they're all the same distance away. In fact, stars are so far away that your eyes can't tell that some stars are closer to Earth than others. Scientists use a measurement called a light-year to measure the distance of stars. One light-year is equal to almost 6 trillion miles.

Hadar

320

Proxima Centauri

4

Note: Distances are in light-years and approximate.
The diagram is not to scale.

Acrux

510

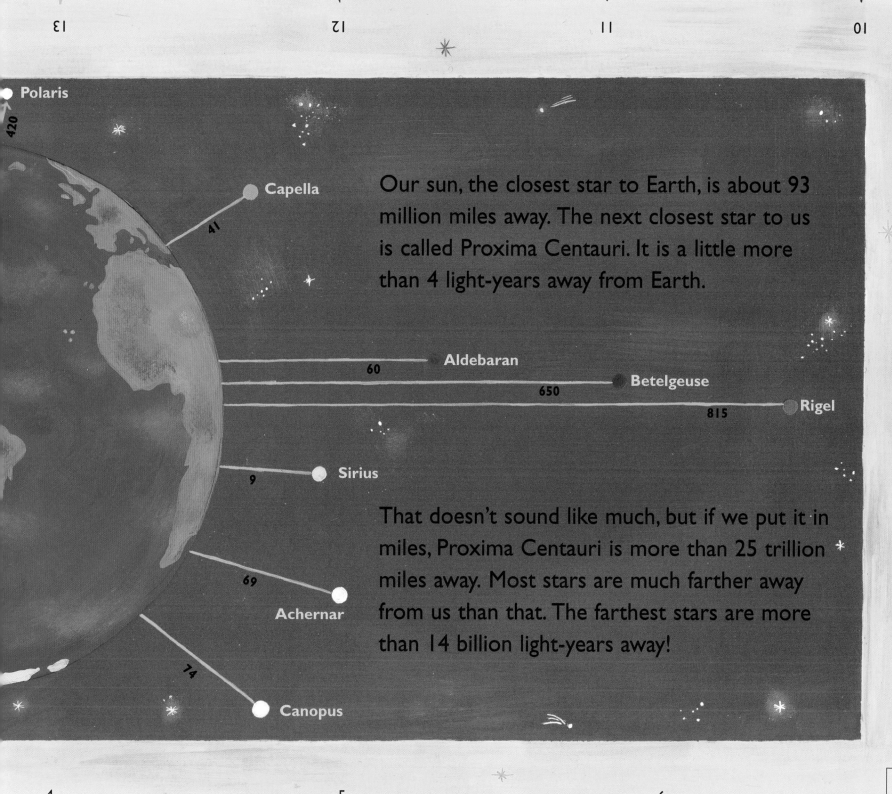

Our sun, the closest star to Earth, is about 93 million miles away. The next closest star to us is called Proxima Centauri. It is a little more than 4 light-years away from Earth.

That doesn't sound like much, but if we put it in miles, Proxima Centauri is more than 25 trillion miles away. Most stars are much farther away from us than that. The farthest stars are more than 14 billion light-years away!

Polaris
420

Capella
41

Aldebaran
60

Betelgeuse
650

Rigel
815

Sirius
9

Achernar
69

Canopus
74

Brightness:

Size, Color, Temperatur

Not all stars are the same. You've probably noticed that some stars look bright and some look dim. Some stars look bright because they are very, very hot. Other stars look bright because they are very, very big. Some stars, like our sun, look bright because they are close to Earth.

This can be confusing. It means that a small, hot star that is far away can look dimmer than a cool, big star that is closer to Earth. Astronomers, scientists who study stars, look for other clues besides brightness to learn what a star is like.

One clue that astronomers use is the color of a star. Most stars look white at first. But if you go where it's really dark and look carefully, you'll see that some stars are red, some are yellow, some really are white, and some are even blue.

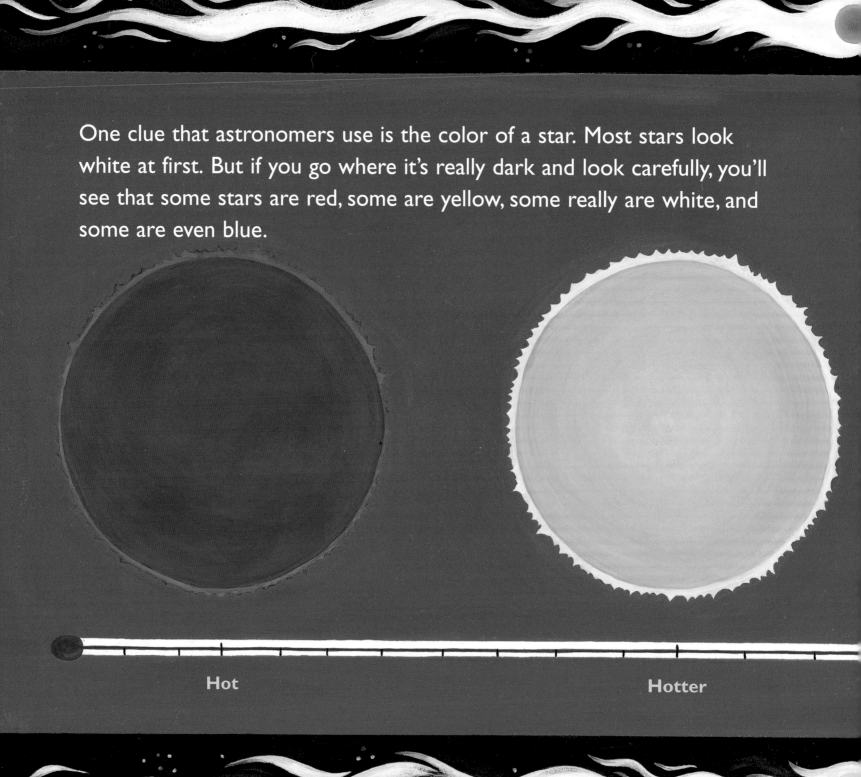

Hot   Hotter

Red stars are hot, white stars are very hot. Blue stars are very, very hot! Our sun is a yellow star. Yellow stars are in between red stars and white stars in temperature. Where would our sun fall on the chart below?

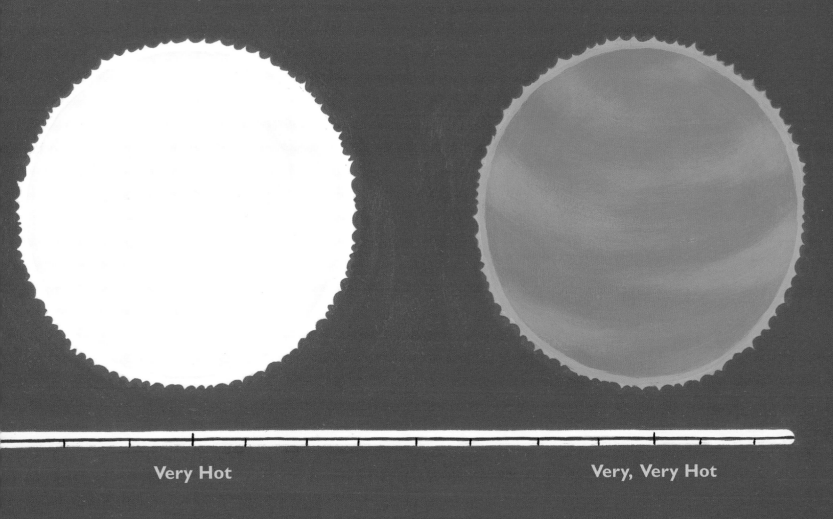

Very Hot   Very, Very Hot

Libra

Scorpius

Leo

Gemini

Taurus

In ancient times, people saw patterns in the stars.
You also can use the stars to imagine pictures,
just like playing connect the dots. These pictures
made out of stars are called constellations.

North Pole

Sagittarius

Capricornus

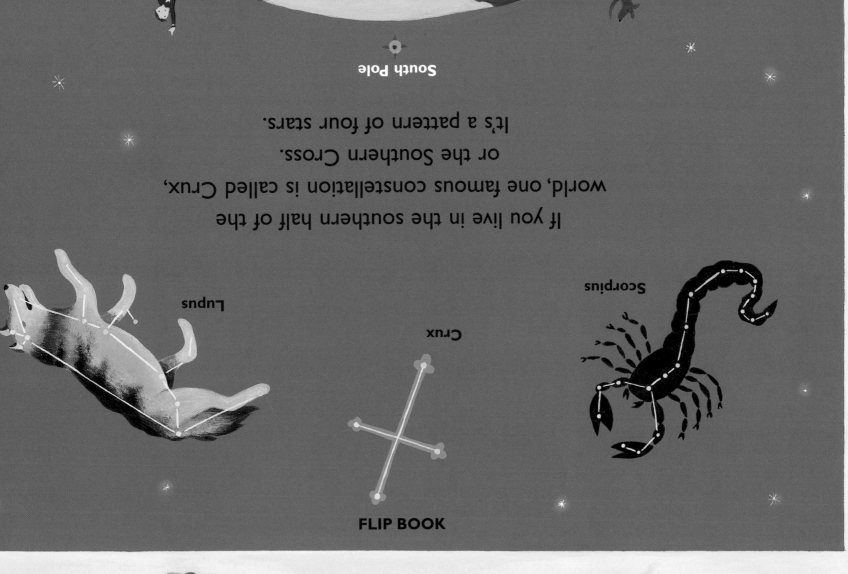

Taurus

South Pole

If you live in the southern half of the
world, one famous constellation is called Crux,
or the Southern Cross.
It's a pattern of four stars.

Lupus

Crux

Scorpius

Aries

FLIP BOOK

Aquarius

Pisces

Orion, the hunter, is another famous constellation. If you live in the northern half of the world, Orion is easy to find in the evening sky during the winter. Just look for three stars in a row. These three stars make up Orion's belt. Then you can trace the rest of Orion.

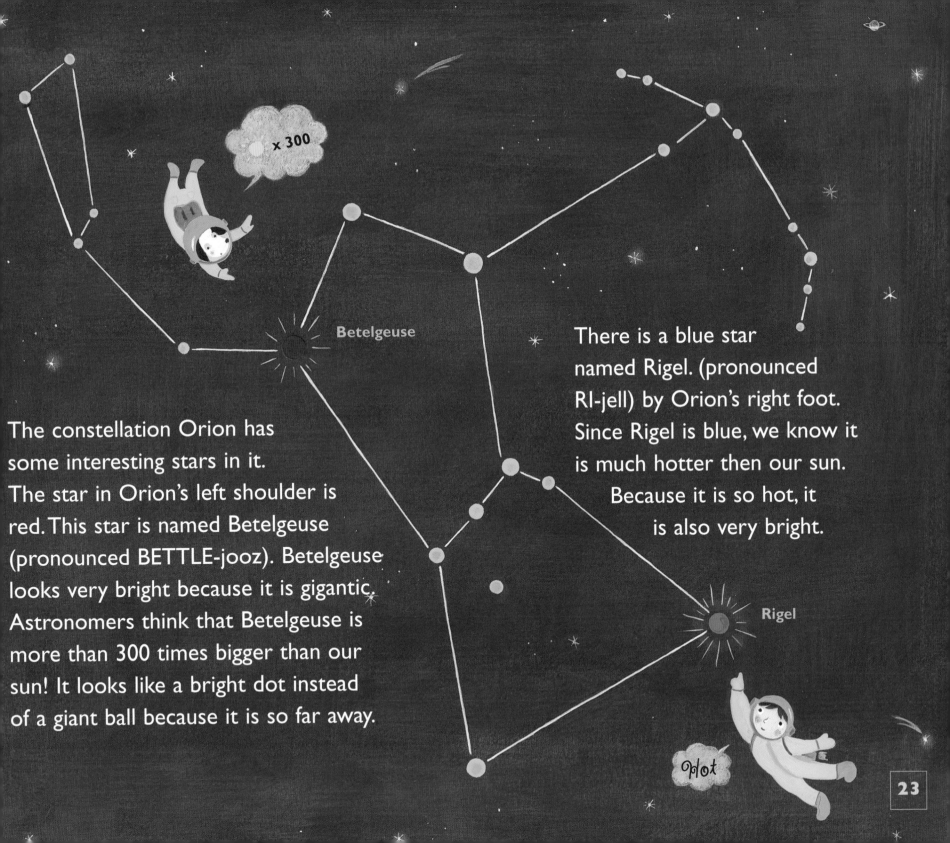

x 300

Betelgeuse

The constellation Orion has some interesting stars in it. The star in Orion's left shoulder is red. This star is named Betelgeuse (pronounced BETTLE-jooz). Betelgeuse looks very bright because it is gigantic. Astronomers think that Betelgeuse is more than 300 times bigger than our sun! It looks like a bright dot instead of a giant ball because it is so far away.

There is a blue star named Rigel. (pronounced RI-jell) by Orion's right foot. Since Rigel is blue, we know it is much hotter then our sun. Because it is so hot, it is also very bright.

Rigel

hot

If you watch the night sky for a few hours, you'll see that stars seem to move slowly across the sky. They all seem to move together and the patterns of the constellations don't change. Just like our sun, stars rise in the east and set in the west.

EAST

noon

4:00 P.M.

8:00 P.M.

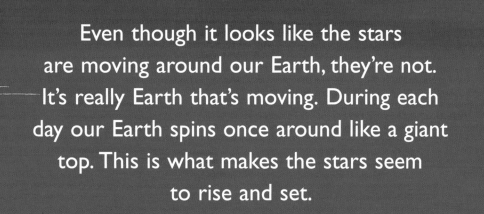

Even though it looks like the stars
are moving around our Earth, they're not.
It's really Earth that's moving. During each
day our Earth spins once around like a giant
top. This is what makes the stars seem
to rise and set.

N

WEST

S

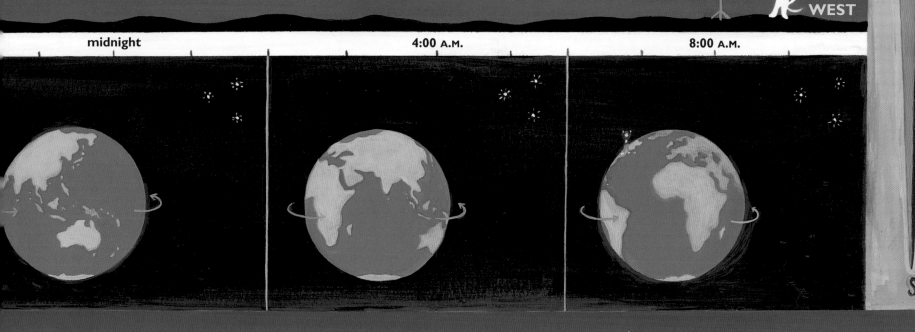

midnight   4:00 A.M.   8:00 A.M.

In the northern part of the world you can see one star that never seems to move. This star is called Polaris. Polaris is also known by another name. It is called the North Star because it's always found in the northern part of the sky.

10:00 p.m.

Sunset

Long ago, people discovered that they could use it to find their direction here on Earth. Many people think the North Star is one of the brightest stars. It's not.

To find the North Star, you can use a simple trick. First find seven stars that make the shape of a ladle. This pattern is called the "Big Dipper." Follow the last two stars in the bowl of the Big Dipper. They will lead you straight to the North Star.

Sunrise

2:00 a.m.

There is no "South Star." People who live in the southern part of the world use the Southern Cross to help guide them.

Some stars are big. Some stars are bright. All stars are made of hot glowing gas, just like our sun. The sun is our star, the only one near our Earth.

Searching for Life

When you wish upon a star, you're really
wishing on a far-off sun. And that sun might have a
planet just like our Earth going around it. Who knows,
maybe someone on a planet going around another star
is looking at our sun, wishing upon our star!

Hello

Star Light, Star Bright

You can experiment to see how the distance to a star seems to change its brightness.

Here's what you'll need:

- 2 flashlights that are about the same brightness
- 2 friends to help
- A big dark room

① Make the room as dark as possible. Give each friend a flashlight. Have them turn the flashlights on.

② Ask your friends to stand about 10 feet from you and point the flashlights at you. How bright does the light from the two flashlights look?

Do not open

③ Ask one friend to walk backward while the other one stands still. What effect does moving farther away have on the brightness of the light?

④ Now ask the friend who didn't move to take a few steps toward you. How does moving closer affect the brightness of the light?

⑤ Which light seems brighter, the one that is closer or the one that is farther away? What does this tell you about the connection between distance and the brightness of stars?

What did you discover? (use a mirror to read)

When you start, both flashlights are the same distance away. As the first flashlight moves away, its light seems to get dimmer. As the second flashlight gets closer to you, its light seems to get brighter.

Think of the two flashlights as stars that are the same in size and brightness. The flashlight close to you is our sun. The flashlight far from you is a more dista star. The sun flashlight is no bigger or brighter than the other star flashlight, but is closer so it looks brighter.

When flashlight gets clos

Think

The artist created her art in acrylics and mixed media.

Book design by LeSales Dunworth
The text is set in Gill Sans. The display type is Clover.

Jump Into Science series consultant:
Christine Kiel, Early Education Science Specialist

Library of Congress Cataloging-in-Publication Data

Tomecek, Steve.
Stars / by Stephen M. Tomecek ; illustrated by Sachiko Yoshikawa.
p. cm.—(Jump into science)
Summary: Introduces stars and what they are made of, how they shine,
their positions with relation to earth, and more.
ISBN 0-7922-8203-5 (hard cover)
ISBN: 0-7922-5581-X (paperback)
1. Stars—Juvenile literature. [1. Stars.] I. Yoshikawa, Sachiko,
ill. II. Title. III. Series.
QB801.7 .T66 2003
523.8—dc21
2001007551

Hardcover ISBN: 978-0-7922-6955-7
Trade paperback ISBN: 978-0-7922-5581-9

Steve Tomecek
is the Executive Director and founder
of Science Plus, Inc. He is the author
of three other Jump Into Science books
as well as several other titles, including
the winner of the 1996 American
Institute of Physics Excellence in Science
Writing Award. He lives in
Bellerose, New York.

Sachiko Yoshikawa
moved to San Francisco from Japan
in 1988 to study art. She works in
mixed media, with vibrant collage,
and in web-based animation.
Sachiko lives in Oregon. This is her first
picture book for children.

Since 1888, the National Geographic Society has funded more than 12,000 research,
exploration, and preservation projects around the world. The Society receives funds
from National Geographic Partners, LLC, funded in part by your purchase.
A portion of the proceeds from this book supports this vital work.
To learn more, visit natgeo.com/info.

NATIONAL GEOGRAPHIC and Yellow Border Design are trademarks of the
National Geographic Society, used under license.

For more information, please visit nationalgeographic.com,
call 1-877-873-6846, or write to the following address:

NATIONAL GEOGRAPHIC PARTNERS
1145 17th Street N.W.
Washington, D.C. 20036-4688 U.S.A.

First paperback printing 2006

Printed in the United States of America
22/QCG/10